DATE DUE

Material World

CHANGING MATERIALS

Robert Snedden

Heinemann Library
Chicago, Illinois

Designed by Celia Floyd
Originated by Dot Gradations
Printed by Wing King Tong, Hong Kong

05 04 03 02 01
10 9 8 7 6 5 4 3 2 1

Library of Congress Cataloging-in-Publication Data
Snedden, Robert.
Changing materials / Robert Snedden.
      p. cm. -- (Material world)
   Includes bibliographical references and index.
   ISBN 1-58810-069-3 (library binding)
   1. Chemical reactions--Juvenile literature. 2. Strength of materials--Juvenile literature. [1. Chemical reactions. 2. Strength of materials.] I. Title.
QD501 .S678 2001
541.3'9--dc21

                                                                00-061342

Acknowledgments
The author and publishers are grateful to the following for permission to reproduce copyright material: Actionplus/P. Millereau, p. 5; Andrew Lambert, pp. 18, 26; Environmental Images/Vanessa Miles, p. 16; Environmental Picture Library/Pete Addis, p. 19; Environmental Picture Library/Leslie Garland, pp. 7, 24; Network/Barry Lewis, p. 21; Sally and Richard Greenhill, p. 20; Science Photo Library/Martin Bond, p. 4; Science Photo Library/Charles D. Winters, p. 10; Rosenfeld Images Ltd, p. 11; Rosenfeld Images Ltd/John Greim, p. 12; Tony Stone Images/David Hoffman, p. 8; Tony Stone Images/Christopher Bissell, p. 22; Tony Stone Images/Robert Yager, p. 23; Tony Stone Images/Matthew McVay, p. 29.

Cover photograph Tony Stone Images/Johan Elzenga.

Every effort has been made to contact copyright holders of any material reproduced in this book. Any omissions will be rectified in subsequent printings if notice is given to the publisher.

Some words are shown in bold, **like this.** You can find out what they mean by looking in the glossary.

Contents

A World of Change

Many of the materials we use are thrown away after only being used once.

None of the objects around us remain unchanged over time. You have seen how things get broken, batteries go dead, clothes wear out, and food goes bad. These materials, and all the other materials we use, are acted upon by many outside forces.

The right choice

Some materials are designed to be used just once, such as the tissue you use for blowing your nose on. Others materials have to last longer. It would be incredibly wasteful and expensive to have to buy a new set of clothes every day—that rules out the use of tissue for clothing! When a materials scientist sets out to choose a material for a particular purpose, it is important to know the conditions that the material is likely to meet.

Chemical changes

There are few materials that do not react in some way with their environment. Coming into contact with other materials can cause chemical changes to take place. For example, iron rusts if it comes into contact with the air, and so has to be protected. Kitchen utensils have to be made from materials that will not react with the foods they touch. A car battery has to be made of a material that can withstand the **acid** it contains. A materials scientist has to know the chemical characteristics of a material in order to know how it will react with the other materials it could meet during everyday use.

Physical forces

The materials we use are affected by physical forces too, such as changes in temperature, stresses, and **pressure.** The extent of these forces depends on the job a material has to do.

Raw materials

Knowing how materials react to change is not only important to the way they are used, but also to the way in which they are manufactured or obtained from **raw materials.** For example, plastics and glass are made from chemicals and molded into shape, while metals have to be extracted from **ores.** Materials scientists are always looking for ways to make new and improved materials. Understanding how they change is fundamental to that search.

A glass bicycle might look beautiful, but what would happen the first time it hit a bump? A new material must be given a series of tests to make sure that it can perform the job it is needed for.

Chemical Reactions

A **chemical reaction** takes place when two or more substances react together to form new substances. Chemical reactions are different from the physical changes that can take place in a material. In a physical change, such as melting or freezing, the **atoms** making up the substance are still joined together in the same way, whether it is a solid, liquid, or gas.

When two substances react together, the bonds that hold the atoms together are broken and reformed to make new substances.

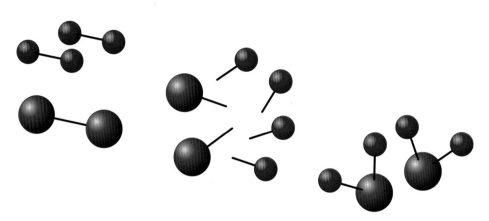

Breaking the bonds

For a chemical reaction to take place, the **bonds** that hold atoms together have to be broken and reformed in a different way. Chemical reactions can be slow, such as when iron combines with oxygen to form rust, or very fast, as in an explosion. Most chemical reactions produce heat, although some need heat to get started.

Chemical equations

When a chemical reaction takes place it seems that one substance has disappeared to be replaced by a new substance. Although the new substance might look totally different, the total number of atoms present does not change. In a chemical reaction, matter is neither created nor destroyed. Chemists use chemical equations to show what occurs in chemical reactions.

For example, a chemist would write down rusting like this:

$$4Fe + 3O_2 = 2Fe_2O_3$$
iron + oxygen = iron oxide (rust)

The equation shows how iron reacts with oxygen gas to form solid rust. The chemical formula for rust is Fe_2O_3. A chemical formula is a group of letters and numbers that tells us how many atoms of each **element** are combined in a **compound**. What it means in this equation is that four atoms of iron (Fe) combine with three **molecules** of oxygen (each made up of two oxygen atoms) to form two molecules of iron oxide, the chemical name for rust.

The substances on the left of the equation are called the reactants. The reactants are the substances that take part in a chemical reaction. In other words, they are the ones that are changed. Chemists have worked out the proportions of atoms involved in chemical reactions by carefully measuring the amounts of each reactant involved. You can see that there are ten atoms in total (four iron and six oxygen). The material on the right of the equation is called the product. It is the result of the reaction. Some reactions have more than one product. In this case there is only one product, rust. Add up the atoms on the right and you will see that the product also contains ten atoms. There are two molecules of iron oxide, each made up of two iron atoms and three oxygen atoms.

If iron is left exposed to the air, it will react with oxygen to form rust. Covering it with a protective coat of zinc can help prevent rusting from happening.

Reaction Rates

It is important to know how materials will react when they are brought together. Some chemicals can react together very rapidly, producing a great deal of energy. This could be dangerous if it happened unexpectedly.

Chemical kinetics

The branch of chemistry that investigates the rates of **chemical reactions** is called chemical kinetics. The word "kinetic" means moving. **Kinetic energy** is the energy of movement. In order for chemicals to react together, the **molecules** that make them up have to be moving so they can collide with each other. If the molecules bang together with enough force, the **bonds** holding them together can be broken and reformed to make new **compounds.** The **atoms** in a solid move much less than those in a liquid or a gas— they just vibrate while staying in the same position. In a reaction such as rusting, which involves a solid, collisions with enough energy do not happen very often and thus iron rusts slowly.

An explosion takes place as a result of a very rapid and highly energetic chemical reaction.

Changing the rate

There are various ways in which the rate of a reaction can be changed. Heating the chemicals involved in the reaction gives the molecules more kinetic energy, increasing the chances of collisions taking place. On the other hand, cooling the reactants slows down the movement of the molecules, cutting down on the number of collisions. This is why freezing food is a good way of preventing it from going bad.

The size of the **particles** involved in the reaction is also important. The smaller the particles, the greater the **surface area**. The greater the surface area, the more there is of the material to take part in a reaction. Grinding something up very finely increases the total surface area. A large piece of wood will burn fairly slowly and steadily since it has a relatively small surface area in relation to its **volume**. However, the same amount of wood ground up to form wood chips will have a larger total surface area and will burn rapidly if it is thrown into a flame.

Try it!

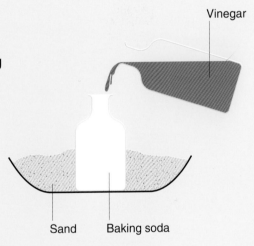

Vinegar

Sand   Baking soda

What will the reaction rate be when mixing baking soda with vinegar?

You will need

sand
water
vinegar
baking soda

red food coloring
a large dish
a small plastic bottle

1. Add some food coloring to the vinegar.
2. Fill the bottle halfway with water and dissolve a couple of teaspoons of baking soda in it.
3. Pile sand around the bottle to make a volcano cone, leaving the top of the bottle uncovered. Now pour the red vinegar into the bottle and watch your volcano erupt!

Was this a fast or slow reaction rate?

Metal Reactions

Metals can be ordered in a **reactivity series** that allows chemists and materials scientists to predict how they will react with each other and with other chemicals.

Reactivity series

The reactivity series is a list for metals—with the most reactive metal at the top and the least reactive at the bottom. There are never any surprises in the reactivity series. Metals at the top will always react more strongly than metals at the bottom. Some metals, such as potassium, are so reactive that they are never found as pure metals in nature. Potassium was only discovered in 1807 when electricity was first used to separate materials. Gold, on the other hand, has been known for thousands of years and is highly valued.

Potassium, a highly reactive metal, is never found as a pure **element** in nature and is usually obtained from **ores.**

Steel is often coated in a thin layer of zinc to prevent rusting. This is called galvanization. Zinc is more reactive than steel and will more readily combine with oxygen than steel.

Displacement

In **displacement reactions,** a less reactive element is replaced in a **compound** by a more reactive one. For example, if powdered zinc is added to a **solution** of copper sulfate, the zinc takes the place of the copper metal and forms zinc sulfate instead. This is because zinc is higher in the reactivity series than copper, and therefore more reactive.

The higher a metal is in the reactivity series, the more stable (less reactive) are the compounds that it forms, and so the more difficult it is to extract the pure metal.

*Aluminum, which we think of as very common today, is actually a highly reactive metal that easily **corrodes.** Until chemists found a way of extracting it cheaply in the nineteenth century, it was so difficult to obtain the pure metal that it was more highly valued than gold. The reason why we can use aluminum today, for example in cooking utensils, is that the metal naturally forms a surface coating of unreactive aluminum oxide. This prevents the metal beneath from corroding. If the aluminum oxide were to be removed, then the aluminum would react rapidly with oxygen in the air and corrode.*

Oxidation and Reduction

A breath analysis test is used by police to determine how much alcohol someone has consumed. Alcohol causes an oxidation reaction to take place that makes a chemical in the breath analysis machine change color.

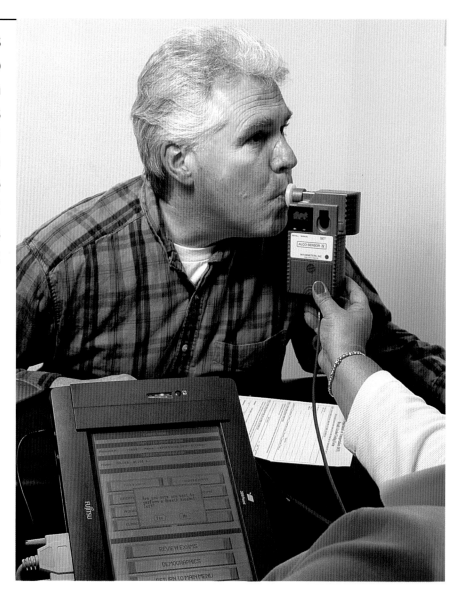

Oxidation is a **chemical reaction** in which a substance combines with oxygen. When you burn something, oxidation is taking place very rapidly. When iron rusts, oxidation is taking place slowly as the iron combines with oxygen from the air. Inside your body, the food you eat is combined with the air you breathe to produce carbon dioxide, water, and energy. This is another example of oxidation.

Chemists have now discovered that some of these reactions can take place without oxygen. Thus, oxidation can be described more generally as a reaction in which **atoms** lose **electrons.**

Redox reactions

The electrons released during oxidation do not just fly off and disappear—they are captured by another substance. This process, by which atoms of an **element** gain electrons, is called **reduction.** Oxidation and reduction always happen together in a balanced reaction, called a **redox reaction.**

Reduction was originally used to describe any chemical reaction in which a substance either combines with hydrogen or loses oxygen.

When iron **ore,** a **compound** of iron and oxygen, is heated with carbon, the carbon acts as a reducing agent. A reducing agent is a substance that removes oxygen or gives electrons. The carbon removes the oxygen from the iron ore, leaving iron behind. The carbon is oxidized and becomes carbon dioxide gas.

Combustion

Combustion is a chemical reaction that usually involves the rapid combination of oxygen with a fuel, producing energy in the form of heat and light. This energy is called the heat of combustion. The fuel may take the form of a solid, liquid, or gas. Combustion occurs, for example, when gas vapor is ignited in a combustion engine—the energy produced is used to move a car. The lowest temperature at which a solid or liquid will catch fire is called its ignition temperature. The ignition temperature and heat of combustion differ from one fuel to another.

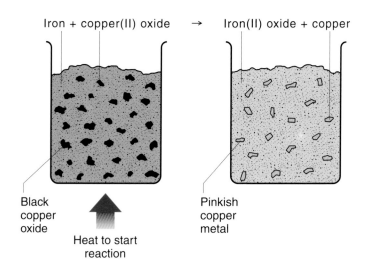

Iron + copper(II) oxide   →   Iron(II) oxide + copper

Black copper oxide

Heat to start reaction

Pinkish copper metal

When powdered iron is heated with copper oxide, the copper oxide is reduced to copper metal and the iron is oxidized to iron oxide.

Catalysts

Catalysts are substances that can alter the rate of a **chemical reaction,** or make the reaction possible, without being changed themselves. In practice, most catalysts are used to speed up reactions. Changing the rate of a reaction by using a catalyst is called catalysis. Catalysis is used in many manufacturing processes, like in the production of synthetic fibers, plastics, and fertilizers. Without the catalysts, the chemical reactions would be too slow to be practical.

Zeolites are catalysts that have a honeycomb structure that traps **molecules** while they react with each other. Chemists can make zeolites with different sized holes to suit different reactions.

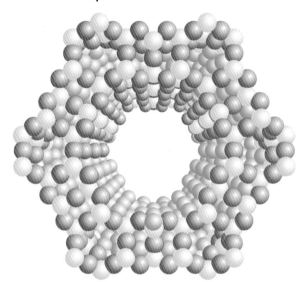

Hydrogenation

*Hydrogenation is a chemical process in which hydrogen is added to a substance. Vegetable oils are often hydrogenated to produce solid fats such as margarine and other butter substitutes. The process is also important in **refining** gasoline. Catalysts are needed to make hydrogenation economical. In 1912, French chemist Paul Sabatier was awarded the Nobel Prize in chemistry for discovering that nickel is a good hydrogenation catalyst.*

How catalysts work

All chemical reactions need energy to get them started. This is called the **activation energy.** Catalysts work by changing the activation energy for a reaction. They do this by providing a new way for the reaction to take place. When the activation energy level is lowered, the reaction rate is increased and the reaction is said to be catalyzed. If the activation energy level is higher, the reaction rate decreases and the reaction is said to be inhibited.

Some substances, called promoters, increase the activity of a catalyst. Other substances can reduce the effects of a catalyst. These are called poisons.

Catalysts and the ozone layer

The pollutant gas nitric oxide acts as a catalyst to break up the **ozone layer** in the earth's upper atmosphere. Normally, an oxygen **atom** and an ozone molecule combine slowly to produce two oxygen molecules. However, in the presence of nitric oxide, a rapid reaction takes place in which nitric oxide molecules combine with oxygen atoms to produce nitrogen dioxide. This then reacts with ozone to form two molecules of oxygen and one molecule of nitric oxide. Over the course of the reaction the amount of nitric oxide does not change. This means that it continues to destroy part of the ozone layer that protects us from the Sun's harmful ultraviolet rays.

Enzymes: natural catalysts

Most of the chemical reactions that take place in living things are ones that have high activation energies. By themselves, they would take place slowly, if at all, but the reactions are speeded up by natural catalysts called **enzymes**. Some enzymes actually increase reaction rates by a billion times more than what they would be normally. Without a catalyst, it would take weeks to convert the food you eat into energy. Just a tiny amount of the enzyme ptyalin, found in saliva, speeds up the reaction so that food can be digested and used to provide energy for your body.

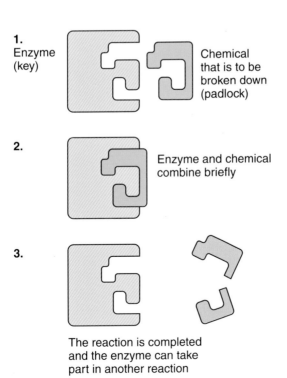

1.
Enzyme (key)

Chemical that is to be broken down (padlock)

2.

Enzyme and chemical combine briefly

3.

The reaction is completed and the enzyme can take part in another reaction

Enzymes work by a "lock and key" mechanism where reacting chemicals combine on the surface of the enzyme.

15

Acids

Acids are found in all sorts of places—carbonated drinks, car batteries, and even in your stomachs. Many acids occur naturally. Hydrochloric acid is produced in your stomach to help digest food. Acids are also widely used in the production of food and drinks, and as preservatives to kill bacteria in food. However, many are poisonous, and strong acids such as sulfuric acid are highly corrosive, which means that they can burn clothes and skin. Acids in rain can damage buildings and kill trees. The chemical industry produces 165 million tons of **corrosive** sulfuric acid a year—it is an essential part of the production of fertilizers, paints, detergents, and other materials.

Acid properties

An acid is one of a group of chemical **compounds** that have certain properties in common. Acids can **dissolve** many metals. **Solutions** of acids have a sour taste and produce a burning sensation if they come into contact with skin.

Acid rain causes a great deal of damage to stone. Some carvings, which had lasted for hundreds of years, have recently been severely eroded by acid rain.

An acid is defined by chemists as a compound that dissolves in water to produce hydrogen **ions** in solution. The strength of an acid depends on how readily it breaks up in solution to form hydrogen ions. For example, when it is dissolved in water, every **molecule** of hydrogen chloride releases a hydrogen ion to form hydrochloric acid. Hydrochloric acid is therefore considered to be a strong acid. Acetic acid, one of the ingredients of vinegar, is a weak acid. It produces only a few hydrogen ions in solution.

Litmus is used as an indicator to test whether liquids are acid or **alkaline.** Litmus is a dye obtained from various **lichens.** Blue litmus paper will turn red if it is brought into contact with an acid.

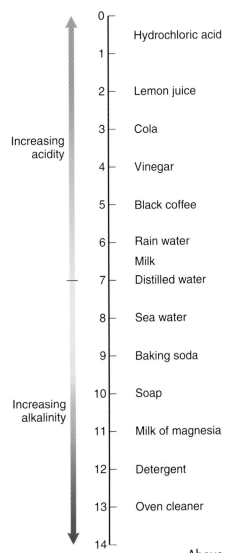

0	Hydrochloric acid
1	
2	Lemon juice
3	Cola
4	Vinegar
5	Black coffee
6	Rain water
	Milk
7	Distilled water
8	Sea water
9	Baking soda
10	Soap
11	Milk of magnesia
12	Detergent
13	Oven cleaner
14	

Increasing acidity

Increasing alkalinity

Above are some common materials and their pHs.

Inorganic and organic acids

Generally, inorganic acids do not contain carbon **atoms.** Many inorganic acids are strong acids and can be highly corrosive. They are used in the production of other chemicals and in the **refining** of crude oil. Sulfuric acid, a strong inorganic acid, is commonly used in car batteries. Other important inorganic acids are hydrochloric acid and nitric acid.

Organic acids are always carbon compounds. They are used in drinks, cosmetics, medicines, and soaps. The first known acid was vinegar, an organic acid. Common organic acids include citric acid, which is found in citrus fruits and ascorbic acid, or vitamin C.

Alkalis

Many common materials contain **alkalis,** including saliva, polishes, and the powdered lime used to neutralize acidic soils. Millions of tons of alkalis are produced every year by the chemical industry. Alkalis have many practical uses. For example, many household oven cleaners contain the alkali sodium hydroxide, which can break down the deposits of fat that build up on the walls of ovens. Magnesium hydroxide is often used as an ingredient in antacids, which are used to treat indigestion caused by excess stomach acidity.

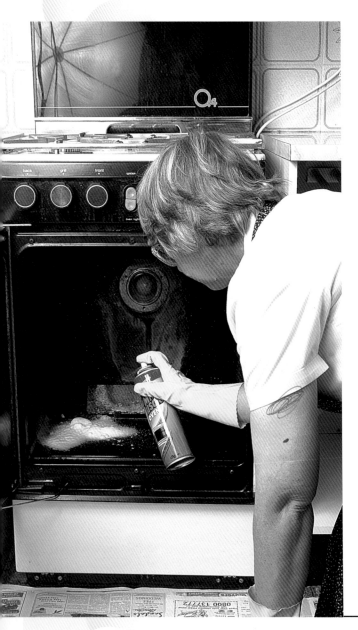

Alkali properties

Alkalis can be divided into strong and weak alkalis. **Solutions** of alkalis all contain the hydroxide **ion** (OH⁻), which gives them a characteristic set of properties. When a strong alkali, such as potassium hydroxide, is **dissolved** in water it **ionizes** completely. This means that it splits into positively **charged** potassium ions (K⁺) and negatively charged hydroxide ions (OH⁻). A weak alkali, such as ammonium hydroxide, is only partially ionized in solution, so there are fewer hydroxide ions. Strong alkalis are just as **corrosive** as strong **acids** and can cause serious burns. Alkalis in solution feel soapy or slippery and have a bitter taste. Red **litmus** paper turns blue if it is brought into contact with an alkali.

Oven cleaners use strong alkalis, like sodium hydroxide, to break down fatty deposits.

A soil that is too acidic will lose essential **nutrients,** so farmers spread the alkali calcium hydroxide (powdered lime) on their fields to neutralize excess acidity.

Neutralization

Whenever an acid and an alkali react together they produce a salt plus water. This process is called neutralization. For example, hydrochloric acid (HCl) and sodium hydroxide (NaOH) give common salt (NaCl) and water (H_2O) when they are mixed together. The equation is:

$$HCl + NaOH = NaCl + H_2O$$

Try it!

Can cabbage indicate whether something is acid or **akaline?**

You will need

red cabbage, chopped
a knife
a saucepan
a large jar

half a liter (one pint) of distilled water
a cutting board
a colander

1. Have an adult boil the distilled water in a saucepan.
2. Remove water from the heat and add the chopped cabbage. Leave until cool.
3. With the colander, strain the purple-red liquid into a jar.

You can use this liquid as an indicator to test whether substances are acid or alkaline. Acids will turn the indicator red and alkalis will turn it green. To test a substance, pour a little of the indicator into a small jar and then add a drop of the substance you are testing. Try lemon juice and vinegar which are weak acids, and milk of magnesia and baking soda which are alkalis.

Do the alkalis and acids you tested have the same effect on the indicator?

WARNING: Always have an adult with you when using the cabbage indicator. Do NOT attempt to test strong alkalis, such as oven-cleaners, or strong acids.

Physical Changes

Ice cream only stays semisolid while it is cold. On a hot day, it will soon melt and drip if you do not eat it quickly!

As we have seen, materials are changed by **chemical reactions.** One material reacts with another and the **atoms** that make them up are rearranged to form something new. On the whole, however, when we use materials we are interested just as much in their physical properties as in their chemical properties. The way in which materials are affected by changes in temperature, in **pressure,** by bending and stretching, and other forces determines how they are used.

Physical properties

Here are just a few examples of how a material's physical properties allow it to be used for different purposes. Glass is very brittle, but it is useful because it is transparent and it can be molded into different shapes when it is molten. Plastics are easy to mold into a limitless variety of shapes. They are lightweight and waterproof, and make ideal containers, although they have the disadvantage of being resistant to chemical attack so they do not breakdown when thrown away. Metals are tough and strong, easily shaped into thin wires or into sheets, good conductors of electricity and heat, and highly reflective when polished. All these physical characteristics make metals very useful materials.

Solubility

Many substances can be **dissolved** in water, or some other liquid, to form a **solution**. These substances are said to be **soluble**. For example, salt can be dissolved in water to give a liquid solution of salt and water. Although the salt may no longer be visible, it has not been changed chemically. Dissolving a substance is a physical change. If the water is removed by **evaporation,** a solid deposit of salt will be left behind.

If a solution of salt in water is allowed to evaporate, deposits of salt crystals are left behind.

Try it!

Will salt and water mix chemically?

You will need
a shallow dish
a beaker
some warm water
table salt

1. Pour the water into the beaker and add salt, stirring until it has dissolved.
2. Pour some of the salt solution into a shallow dish and leave it in a warm place until the water has evaporated.

You will see the salt crystals that have been left behind. Taste a little to prove to yourself that the salt has not been changed by dissolving in the water. This shows that the salt and water did not chemically react with each other.

Stresses and Strains

Stress is a measure of the strength of a force acting on a material. Strain is a measure of the amount by which the object changes shape as a result of that force. Some materials, such as rubber, can change shape easily. Others, such as concrete, do not change shape. If too much stress is put on a material that cannot change shape, it will give way. So stress and strain, for example, are important considerations when choosing materials for constructing buildings and bridges.

An archer pulling back a bow is putting stress on the bow and bowstring. When the string is released, the bow and bowstring will spring back to their original shape.

Elasticity

Sometimes materials are acted on by forces that may make the material change shape because it is not able to move. The ability of an object or material to return to its original size and shape, after being pushed or pulled by an outside force, is called its **elasticity.** All solids have some elasticity. A coiled steel spring and a rubber band are both very elastic, whereas rock is not. No matter how elastic a material is, if the stress applied to the material is great enough it will no longer return to its original shape after the force is removed. Eventually, the material will either break or just not return to its original shape. When this happens, the material is said to have passed its elastic limit.

Elastic energy

When you compress a spring, you are transferring energy into the spring. The energy you are storing there is called **elastic potential energy.** As soon as the spring can return to its original shape the energy will be released. Buildings in earthquake zones are often built on giant springs that can absorb the energy of an earthquake. Building materials like concrete are very inelastic and, if unprotected, the forces produced by an earthquake soon push them past their elastic limit, shattering them.

Concrete structures do not have a great deal of elasticity. The stress of an earthquake can cause them to break and collapse.

Under stress

The higher the stress, the greater the strain. The ratio of stress to strain is called the elastic modulus. It is a measure of how well a material will resist forces acting on it to push it out of shape. A solid with a high elastic modulus, such as steel, has a greater resistance to stress than one with a low elastic modulus, such as rubber.

Temperature Changes

Materials are often exposed to heat. We use heat to cook our food and to warm our homes. In industry, heat is used to **refine** crude oil and to separate metals from their **ores.** Heat is also used to melt materials so that they can be reshaped. Changes in temperature can have many effects on different materials. Metals expand when they get hot and **contract** when they cool.

Temperature and energy

All materials are made up of **atoms** or **molecules** and these are always moving. If they are moving slowly, the material is said to have a low level of **internal energy.** If they are moving rapidly, it has a high level of internal energy. Hot materials have high internal energy levels, cold materials have low levels. Temperature is a measurement of internal energy levels. If a material with a high level of energy comes into contact with a material that has a low level, internal energy passes from high to low until the temperature of both materials is the same. This passage of energy from one object to another is called heat. The water in a hot bath has a high level of internal

Railway engineers learned that metals expanded on hot days, so rail tracks were laid with gaps to allow for this.

energy. If you step into it, it makes you feel warm as heat is transferred to your cooler body. However, if you step into a cold bath your body will have a higher internal energy and heat will flow from you to the bathwater, making you feel rather frigid!

Expanding and contracting

When heat flows into a material, the atoms or molecules take up more space as they move more rapidly and the substance expands. The opposite happens when heat flows out of a material. A thermometer indicates temperature change according to how much the mercury inside it expands and contracts as it heats up or cools down.

Moving heat

Heat moves through a material by **conduction.** If a metal rod is heated at one end, for example, the atoms in the hot end begin to move faster as their internal energy increases. These atoms move faster and strike atoms further along the rod. In this way, the heat travels from atom to atom through the metal.

If the heated metal rod heats the air around it, the heated air expands and rises and cooler air replaces it. The cooler air that is now near the rod becomes warm and, in turn, rises. This flow of heated air moving away from a hot object and cooler air flowing towards it is called a **convection current.** Convection currents carry heat through liquids as well as gases.

Insulating materials

Heat does not easily travel through some materials by conduction. These materials, such as plastic and wood, are called insulators. This is why many cooking utensils have plastic or wooden handles. The metal part of the utensil heats rapidly but the handle stays cool, protecting your hand.

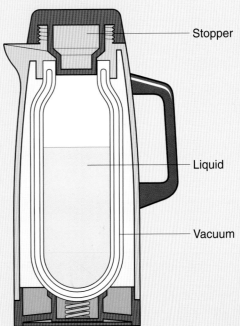

Stopper

Liquid

Vacuum

An insulated beverage container has a vacuum held between two layers to prevent heat from being conducted in or out.

Pressure

Careful consideration has to be given to storing gases. If a gas in a container gets hot, for example, the **pressure** increases and the container might explode. Airplanes that fly high up where the air pressure is very low and submarines that dive beneath the sea where the pressure of the water is very high, both have to be built from materials that can cope with extreme pressure changes.

Blowing up a balloon makes the pressure on the inside greater than the air pressure outside.

What is pressure?

To a scientist, pressure is a force acting on a unit of area on a surface. A force concentrated on a small area produces a greater pressure than the same force acting over a large area. The greater the force, the greater the pressure. In **physics,** the term is usually applied to **fluids.** If a fluid is at rest, pressure is transmitted equally in all directions throughout the fluid. The fluid acts this way because the **molecules** in it can move freely.

The greater the pressure in a gas, the smaller its **volume**. This decrease in volume occurs because the molecules are pushed closer together. Under ordinary conditions, the volume of a gas decreases by half when the pressure doubles. The ability of a gas to compress and expand has many practical uses, for example in its use in car tires that absorb the shock of going over bumps in the road. The volume of liquids and solids also decreases when pressure increases, but by much smaller amounts than for gases.

Air pressure

Air is not very heavy, but there is so much air in the atmosphere that it presses on us from all directions with a pressure of about 14.7 pounds per square inch (1.1 kilograms per square centimeter). The total air pressure on your body probably amounts to thousands of pounds pressing on you. The reason you are not aware of this huge force is because the fluid and air in your body pushes out with an equal, balancing pressure.

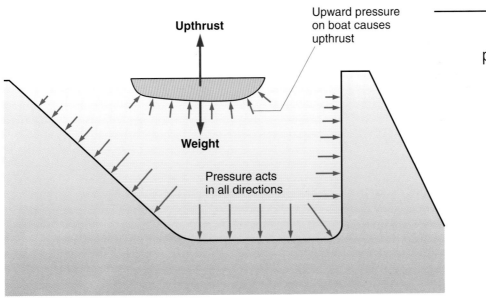

Upward pressure on boat causes upthrust

Upthrust

Weight

Pressure acts in all directions

A liquid exerts pressure evenly in all directions.

Pressure and boiling

The boiling point of a liquid is the temperature at which the pressure of the **vapor** produced is equal to the pressure of the air around it. For water, this is 212°F (100°C) at sea level. With increasing altitude (height), the pressure decreases and the boiling point becomes lower and lower.

Radioactivity

Some materials are composed of **atoms** that are unstable. Over time the atoms break up and become other chemical **elements.** Materials that do this are said to be **radioactive.** The energy produced as these materials decay can be put to use in nuclear power stations and batteries for pacemakers. Radioactive substances change, or decay, at a known rate, so we can work out how old a sample is—for example, radioactive carbon dating is used to tell us how old archaeological artifacts are.

What is radioactivity?

Atoms are made up of clouds of negatively **charged electrons** surrounding a heavier, positively charged **nucleus.** The nucleus of every element except hydrogen consists of **particles** called **protons** and **neutrons.** A normal hydrogen nucleus has just a single proton. Any change in the number of protons in the nucleus produces an atom of a different element. Radioactive substances, such as the elements radium, uranium, and plutonium have very large nuclei and are unstable. They release **radiation** to take on a more stable form. The process of giving off atomic particles is called radioactive decay. As radioactive elements decay, they change into different forms of the same element or into other elements, until finally they reach a point at which they are stable and nonradioactive.

In the course of a lengthy process, radioactive uranium eventually becomes stable.

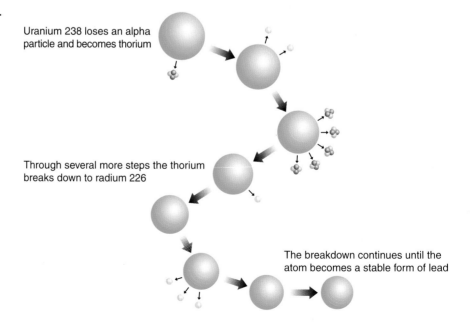

Uranium 238 loses an alpha particle and becomes thorium

Through several more steps the thorium breaks down to radium 226

The breakdown continues until the atom becomes a stable form of lead

Half-lives

The rate of radioactive decay is measured in half-lives. That is the time it takes for one half of the atoms in the radioactive material to decay. This takes place at different rates in different elements or different forms of the same element. Half-lives range from fractions of a second to billions of years.

Particle radiation

When the nucleus of a radioactive element breaks down it can emit radioactivity in a number of different ways. Particle radiation consists of protons, neutrons, and electrons. Alpha particles are fast-moving groups of two protons and two neutrons and are identical to the nuclei of helium atoms. They do not travel far and can easily be stopped by a sheet of paper.

Most alpha particles eventually become atoms of helium gas. Beta particles are electrons. They are also fast moving and can travel further than alpha particles. A thin sheet of metal will stop them. Gamma rays are not particles, but a form of high-energy electromagnetic radiation. They are much more difficult to stop and a thick sheet of lead is needed to block them.

Artificial radioactive substances are made by exploding nuclear weapons and in nuclear reactors. These new radioactive atoms are called fission products. Used fuel from nuclear power plants contains many fission products, such as plutonium 239 and barium 140. This used fuel, called nuclear waste, remains hazardous for thousands of years.

Dangerous nuclear waste is continuing to be produced, even though no one has developed a way to properly dispose of it.

Glossary

acid compound that forms hydrogen ions when it dissolves in water

activation energy amount of energy needed for a chemical reaction to begin

alkaline having the properties of an alkali

alkali compound that forms hydroxide ions in solution

atom tiny particle from which all materials are made; the smallest part of an element that can exist

bonds forces that hold atoms together in molecules

catalyst substance that alters the rate of a chemical reaction without itself being changed

charged having an electric charge

chemical reaction reaction that takes place between two or more substances in which energy is given out or taken in and new substances are produced

combustion rapid combination of a substance with oxygen

compound substance that is made up of atoms of two or more elements

condense to change from a gas into a liquid

conduction movement of heat through a solid from an area of high temperature to an area of lower temperature

contract to get smaller

convection current movement of heat through a liquid or gas caused by the tendency of warmer material to rise through colder material

corrode to wear away little by little

displacement reaction reaction in which a more reactive element takes the place of a less reactive element in a compound

dissolve to become incorporated into a liquid and form a solution

elastic potential energy energy stored in a material as a result of its being stretched or compressed; it is released when the material returns to its original shape

elasticity ability of a solid to return to its original shape once distorting forces have been removed

electrons negatively-charged particles that are found in all atoms and that are the main carriers of electrical energy

element substance that cannot be broken down into simpler substances by chemical reactions; an element is made up of just one type of atom

enzyme natural catalyst—a protein that regulates the rate of chemical activity in a living organism

evaporate change into a vapor or a gas

evaporation process by which a liquid turns into a vapor without reaching its boiling point

fluid substance that has no fixed shape; a gas or a liquid

hydrogenation addition of hydrogen to a carbon compound

internal energy energy of movement in the atoms or molecules that make up a substance

ion atom or group of atoms that has an electric charge

ionize atom or molecule that gains or loses electrons and so has an overall electric charge

kinetic energy energy of movement

lichens plants made up of algae and fungus growing together

litmus indicator used to tell whether something is acid or alkaline; litmus turns red in the presence of acid, blue in the presence of alkali

molecule two or more atoms combined together; if the atoms are the same it is an element, if they are different it is a compound

neutron one of the fundamental components of an atom, found in the atom's nucleus; a neutron has no electric charge

nucleus heavy, central part of an atom, made up of protons and neutrons

nutrients substances that are essential for the maintenance of life

ore rock from which metals can be obtained

oxidation chemical reaction in which oxygen combines with a substance, or a reaction in which atoms lose electrons

ozone layer layer in the upper atmosphere formed by molecules of oxygen made up of three oxygen atoms rather than the usual two atoms

particle tiny portion of matter

physics science that deals with the facts about matter and motion

pressure force pushing on a given area

proton one of the fundamental components of an atom, found in the atom's nucleus; a proton has a positive electric charge

radiation high energy rays or particles emitted by radioactive materials

radioactive elements that emit high energy rays and particles

raw material material used in the manufacture of something

reactivity series list of elements ordered by how easily they react with other elements

redox reaction reduction and oxidation occurring together in a reaction

reduction chemical reaction in which a substance loses oxygen, or a reaction in which atoms gain electrons

refine to have impurities removed

soluble able to be dissolved

solution mixture of one substance dissolved in another

surface area measurement of the size of the outermost layer of an object

vapor type of gas

volume amount of space an object takes up

More Books to Read

Barber, Jacqueline. *Chemical Reactions.* Berkeley, Calif.: University of California, Berkeley, Lawrence Hall of Science, 1998.

Fullick, Ann. *Chemicals in Action.* Chicago: Heinemann Library, 1999.

Kerrod, Robin. *Matter & Materials.* Tarrytown, N.Y.: Marshall Cavendish, 1995.

Index